Mixing Cement

Peter Tomassi

Thunder
Rain

FOR MY PARENTS

ACKNOWLEDGMENTS

Grateful acknowledgments are due the editors of the following magazines and journals, in which many of these poems first appeared: *Beauty for Ashes Poetry Review*, "The Trade"; *Central California Poetry Journal*, "Twin Peaks"; *The Comstock Review*, "Boots"; *Gravity*, "Fathers at Echo Lake," "The Trade" as "Mason"; *L'Intrigue*, "The Trade"; *Lynx Eye*, "The Things We Leave"; *Magma - Stukeley Press, London*, "The Trade"; *Paris/Atlantic*, "Rain," "Traveling Carnival Lady" as "Traveling Fair Woman"; *The Pittsburgh Quarterly*, "The Trade"; *Porcupine Literary Arts Magazine*, "Jealousy," "The Thing," "12:17 AM"; PoetryMagazine.com, "Fathers at Echo Lake," "On Leaving," "Outside the Welch House," "Poultry Sale as Poetry Sale," "Parkway Girl"; *Yeast for Food*, "The Trade" as "Pedro's Arms."

Special thanks to Tom McKeown's master ear.

INTRODUCTION

*Nothing will sustain you more than the power to
recognize in your humdrum routine the true poetry of life of the
common-place, of the ordinary man, of the plain, toil-worn
woman, with their loves. . .joys. . . sorrows. . .grief.*
William Osler: *The Student Life.*

Which is exactly why Peter Tomassi has constructed
a cement mixer. He wants to stir others as he has been
stirred. To help us see the gleam in a stranger's eyes as she
tells a story to her child to distract her from the blisters her
ill-fitting shoes are making as the two head for an
anonymous shelter under threat of rain. To help us feel the
cold seeping through a father's glove as he guides his
children's sled, knowing he is so enthralled with their
hilarity and the tilt of their upturned noses that he doesn't
realize his fingers are growing stiff. To help us remember
that pain is less important than the fact that we can feel it
and learn from it. Still see the ermine laid across the snow
by sun and trees or the way the rain diamonds ordinary
cars. Like every real poet, Tomassi mortars images with
surround sound that might otherwise lie forgotten and
unsifted in history's rubble.

'Sand, lime and portland, the musical,' might not feel
like a big accomplishment to a poet convinced that we
"neither destroy nor create, but only shift atoms." But it
puts us close enough to feel the blister rising under the
hammer he once held — the wrench his father gripped as
he gravelled orders to his boy that he did not expect to be
questioned. That it was a hard grip comes through like a
blow. But so does the wonder of being engaged body and
soul in one's work. Feeling an actual building grow. If the
old man barked fit to knock a person's lights out, he shared
his art. Other voices vie — The Fathers of Echo Lake, a
Boy and Girl, a House Wife, a man with ewer ears — but
the stage's foundation (shaky though it sometimes felt,
growing up) is definitely a father-son project. The father's
impatient swagger turns with the spin of a thoughtfully-
wielded trowel to quiet authority, his bellowed orders to a

love letter only just discovered.

Eerie echoes of the clanking, creaking, roaring and whistles that Tchaikovsky'd as Papa lobbed looks at the kid (would Pete never learn?) for dropping the lime again reverberated in grownup Peter's ears as he struggled to freshen his mortar and steady his level. A baseball park requires a lot of piles, and the San Francisco Giants' new coliseum is no exception.   In every clank and bellow, an old haunt lay in wait: Lower East Side, for instance. (". . .Dominicans, Italians, smart-mouthed Bay Ridge girls, the indomitable Hasidim. . .")

The sand, lime and portland comes from something the poet said as he struggled to pinpoint the absurdities and frustrations of modern-day employment, whether it be writing deodorant ads, dreaming up pricey software or touting Tupperware. "We all spend our days mixing cement," he pointed out. How many of us are glued to a clock-clogged treadmill, endlessly repeating, repeating, repeating? Never complete anything, or feel we are meant to? What would it be, we ask ourselves over endless drinks or when 3 a.m. ghosts bolt us upright in our beds, to make something we could point to with pride? Something of benefit. Something. . .concrete.

To make concrete, you must listen to your instructor, measure with care and keep your tools in order. As with life's poetry, the rules are quite simple. Watch the details and respect your ingredients. Make sure the timing's right and don' let Nobody mess with your mess. But once the mix is in, hey! Time to check out the scenery and catch up on kith and kin. After all, who needs a building or a sidewalk or a bridge — pen, computer, canopener, Giants' tee — unless the people for whom they are meant give a fig? These are only a few of the questions Mixing Cement tends to prompt.

Let us hope for many more life poems from mix-master Peter Tomassi.

Phyllis Jean Green, November 1999

Contents

CEMENT

The Trade 2

Writer 4

Fathers at Echo Lake 6

Dinner with Pedro 7

Wanderlust Court 9

Boy and Girl 10

Milestone 12

Amalia 13

Missionaries 15

Mortar 16

SAND

Beginning of a Song 18

Outside the Welch House 18

Boots 19

12:17 am 20

Fetch 21

Parkway Girl 22

The House of Moses 23

New Year 25

At a Window 26

Traveling Carnival Lady 27

Man And Woman 29

The Things We Leave 32

WATER

Morning Pen 34

Rain 34

Prometheus 35

Twin Peaks 36

The Thing 38

Early December 39

Backyard Orpheus 40

The Rose 41

House Wife 43

Entrance 44

LIME

Builders in Toms River 46

The Art 47

Jealousy 48

On Leaving 50

Poem 52

End of the World 54

To Bruegel the Elder 55

Judgment 56

Rear View 57

Song 59

On Common Man 60

Poultry Sale 62

Cement

THE TRADE

His papier-mâché legs
Stand on footings dripping mortar,
Like pigeon droppings
Immortalized in concrete.
His mornings begin
On simple monuments.

To the footing I bring new blocks
The shape of cigar butts stepped on.
He lectures on water and the trade:
My back for forearms like giant squash,
My hands for mitts that catch cut stone.

It's a planter we are replacing.
Rows of gray, dark gray, gray,
Mortar, block, mortar, block, mortar,
Knocking them to plumb.
It is the rows we are building only,
Making clean flush tract
Cured in morning sweat
As if he would own it,
As if sweating were owning.

I watch – yawning – his cement-gray hands
Growing hard –
Fingers squeeze purple from the brick tongs,
Streak in the plumb chalk's yellow.

I see me in the cementy soup:
Arms sinewless,
Stout, smooth gourds, waiting to hatch
Rivulets of olive muscle,
Mounds of weedy Italian landscape,
Molded concrete curves
Speckled with black cancers.

2

He leaves a scored brick,
Grabbing the cup as he coughs.
He has caught me again.
Staring down his cup of coffee,
Working.

WRITER

You're putting on airs again:
    Piss, exhaust, month-old sweat,
Sweeter somehow than the suit and briefcase
    That pressed me on the sidewalk.

They pull me headlong toward your skin:
Craters that have swallowed whole histories,
Inhaled truckloads of Thunderbird.

A Death Valley takes the first soaking,
You're curled *in vitro*,
Dried up there,
Sandblasted,
Legs hammered into fender chrome
    Waffling in the junkyard heat.

A body is reincarnated from the chimney sweep
Squatting there day after day,
Ancient in its black,

Scribbling on a rolled up newspaper,
Pen curled in hand,
Coveting secrets of night downtown.

If I look closely I can see us, dear friend,
Writing the same grotesque chronicles:
You made some rock paintings once.
And your journals –
They did not find the quill and parchment

Fossilized deep in a subway arctic,
Nor did they
    Your typewriter,
Long since reclaimed by the steelmongers.

All that was left
Was this foundering word processor,
A slick beige printer,
Its insides vomiting
Scraps of old newsprint.

FATHERS AT ECHO LAKE

Wind sledded in wet gloves
Molded to the rails
Of Flexible Flyers,

A whir against spiky kid shouts,
Air ripping feather-packed nylon,
The hushed worry of fathers
Bogged down in corduroy.

Sharp trails in their collared faces
Wrapped up in plaid scarves that flapped
Pennants hurrying the onslaught.
Unruly little bulls,

Children take over from the herders,
Fists and shouts riding
The delirium of fathers' crises,
Of briefcases that empty, fill, empty.

The aging men reach for firmness
In slick ice footings
Beneath powdery soft
Landings of snow fallen thick.

A few fat drops like bricks.
The call of engines
Bark in the parking lot,
And paneled wagons glide away,
Down toward safety,
The wet ice.

Dinner with Pedro

Down a street built.up from extras
In a road-metal, two-by-four room
Squats a cigar couch,
Gutted Soviet television,
A teetering shelf stuffed with maps.
Pedro Larrando, my dinner host,

Watches his wife's fingers teach my companion's
Never to trim pork, the revolutions of *arroz congri*,
A secret lost on oil-patched cheeks that dry
Only asleep, when the hot spineless wind
Shepherds in fresh Cuban salt.

In his face, a mirror, my friend's thighs.
It makes sense.
All men secretly love the same kind of pornography,
A blend of flesh carved from stone and old fashion magazines
To which he is all complement, bits the sculptor cast aside
And sewed loosely into ancient Spanish leather.

Here, where stomachs are atheists,
His hangs a wise, lumpy Buddha,
Everything ever read or eaten sacked
By a white T-shirt, a wide-waisted pair of gringo jeans.
We begin to smell dinner.

Wriggling spindles that twist in his scalp squirm
Clear across bald. Excited by the guidebook we have fed,
They stir to feel the currents
To see once more fields of *Habana Nueva*
Bare as his suede arms are hairless,
The seeds too cramped to grow.

I follow a trunk to branches to thin fingers
Tipping the pages up and down.
Maps of the old Americas
Are a year of inedible dreams,
Words in the stomach.

Wanderlust Court

You have your moments, Mr. Street.
Tucked away like a disease, quarantined
To through traffic.
Still your hallmarks managed
Travel – the pink swirl
Of cat faces stitched to porch flags,
The landscaper's carved shrubs,
The house pets and garden gnomes
You share with the avenues.

You defined travel, your occupants might have said.
Ideas a cross-stitch of neighborhood patterns
From Summit Ave, Sandra Circle –
A brigade of like-minded door knockers,
Antique milk boxes choked with spider webs.
The snap of Toyota mauve.

You were visited rarely by the curious:
Junk seekers, hobos who walked your path
Without dog or child, alone,
Without any good reason but perversion.
They made you
Cover your bare walks,
Thicken your hedge.

And then there were the invited
Block partiers, carolers. When the postman
Saw you in your robe and boxers
Repacking the garage at noon
You greeted him like one of your bushes.

Put down your bags,
Some new company is arriving.
Time you left your stoop.

Boy and Girl

In the grapple
Of fire escape and roof tar
They chase each other,
Ripped T-shirt
To scuffed knee,
Sun-burnt shoulder
To sticky flip-flop.

The clouds split
On cotton toes
Like spent lovers
Working up surprises
For their reunion.
They wind themselves
Into tornadoes
Of thick cotton candy,
Releasing the children sweetly
To a wedge of fenced dirt
Between their tenement
And the estate below.

Boy and girl pretend
To dig for water
With the old neighbor's
Toothless rake,
Imagining a private spring
They'll hide with plastic,
Returning each day
To new child-god myths.

They laugh as they burrow
The slim topsoil
Revealing trinkets and gems
Meant to guide them

To the oasis. They hear
Their own laughter
In bursts of quick air,
Trickles of wood on rock,

The sinful call
Of a white-capped neighbor
Leaping the fence
With an offer to rake –
For cookies.

They refuse,
Claiming their fortunes
In mud cakes instead,
In wet backyard heirlooms
Collected by a house of wind.

MILESTONE

Of a boulder I came upon
To the side of the highway,
Like a small erudite mountain
Seated neatly in chicken wire,
The Shell station's neon
For a reading lamp,
I can only wonder

How, skinned from the glacier's knee,
It glimpsed Noah, helpless to act,
Or how it might still
Resent the hasty sale of Carteret,
Washington's frown after the Hessians,
The race riots in Newark's belly,
The shine of cheap car suits,
An artist who tattooed
Jesus was here 4/99,

If the last two million years
Compare to me
Hurrying the pump with my watch,

How a thousand patient shards,
Like sharp starving mouths,
Crave the next hero snowflake.

AMALIA

You said when you drink red wine
You remember your grandmother
Crushing grapes between her toes,
Tony Bennett rising from a loudspeaker.

Ida – Amalia far too big a name –
Began to disappear about the time you turned ten,
Watching her teeter on a stepladder
To steer a jug of bleach into the washer.

    You could see her, right over her head,
Inhaling fumes that would seal the family name
By the rims of her lungs, the rubber in her arches,
Tipping a pastry neck above the machine
To conduct the whirlpool of cottonwater and soil.

    It was true
Your grandfather had long since forgotten
The must of dirty clothes,
Had stopped smelling the blend of sour grapes
And Clorox about her like a cloud,

Had stopped wondering about her sleeves limping:
Ida had stopped using her cabinets.
Amalia was losing syllables, decibels,
Her mouth shrinking to a pair of raisins.

The folds in her skin wrinkled a soft hilly sheet,
Olive Italian bluffs that sheltered the town of her youth
As a blanket strewn about for drying,
Its satin folds wet from too much Rose Milk.

Up the basement stairs – Ida seemed to come only up –
Her stride was hard and arthritic.
When she emerged a kiss of white laundry
Held forth like an offering to Bacchus –
She slid-stepped through the kitchen to her room

13

And returned to greet you in washed-out house clothes
Red-faced like the last maid to the king of Sicily.

Then she was gone.

MISSIONARIES
for W. H. Auden

The recruiters came ashore
Out of their hollow trucks,
Hard-looking 25-ish boys
Who read the sports section,
One Mets game in July
Bigger than ten Desert Storms.

They sat with Penthouse waiting,
Sticky paneled walls to each side
An Indian grocery, Chinese laundromat,
Proprietors with a future all their own.
They are not here to produce
They are here clocking minutes.

The hawker and the Jehovah's Witness
Who rouse them with junk,
Dropping leaflets with wooden shrugs,
Have at least what passes for aim.
They neither make nor sell –
It's no wonder they drink before breakfast.

But their iron ships on the seared black
Macadam of the Marines' parking lot
Seem to gain from having nothing to do.
Without a human plan
To tell them whom to kill
Their structures are kind,

And, far from looking lost,
Appear as if they were meant
To be there, stalked by opinion,
Steel cages bowing in the heat,
Unformed, waiting in that green
Until their history can be filled.

MORTAR

Lightning!
    What I thought were my hands
Are a pair of mason's trowels.

Sand

BEGINNING OF A SONG

The night has begun
So start the moon

And switch on Big Dipper,
Who having watched civilly
For those other towns
Is about ready
For our dance.

OUTSIDE THE WELCH HOUSE

Here it is at sunrise
Resembling an old desk
Left for ruin in the weeds out back,
Clapboard drawers warped to their runners,
Top stained from dewy elbows and cat,
Running-down blood from empty nail holes.
It absorbs the highway's first truck
With a rattle of its knobs.

Here is the form of sinewy America
Who lies there, big-eyed
Ornery child-beast
Fondling his sharp-edged toys,
So well trussed and riveted
Our veneer complaints
Leave him only louder, crankier,
Clacking his cinders,
Left to explain himself
To the weeds out back.

BOOTS

I followed his heels around the stone yard,
The hardware store, the lumber depot,
A rabble of oversized shoes and laundry.
Flannel cast awkwardly from the family mold.

I followed his soles up scaffolds, up stairs.
Followed the jagged imprints of crunched asphalt,
Spidering beneath flinty remnants,
Dried gray soup from pregnant cement trucks.

I would have followed that light-coffee leather
Up the shells of chimneys were I allowed,
If my hands were not so slight I could have
Gripped rooftops, looking down on the things

He framed in boxes: patios, front porches, stone planters.
It was great he would say, clutching a trowel
As Zeus might have, doling out mortal rewards.
Because even life could be churned in sand, cement, lime,

A solid pair of boots. This was our history together.

Walking from our room full of guests
I passed them just now,
Slouching there unearthed
By the heater coils,
Before the kitchen linoleum
Winds to knotted shag,
          Waiting
Waiting, for them to wake.

12:17 AM

I guess you won't be coming home.
And there was so much today:

A man on the street
Harnessed to twelve garbage bags
Full of cans and bottles
Seemed to be talking to me
(But no)
Sweetly from cracked yellow lips,
Mouthing the cold air,
Thanking it
For the quiet chatter.

A gray-haired couple
Stopped to offer their empty Coke.
Then walked on. Not a word.

At the bus stop
A mother sat with her baby
Rocking the old stroller,
Its canopy zipper stuck,
Safety strap stretched to eight-year-old.
She held her mouth in her coat
As the shelter spoke the minutes late
With beaten Plexiglas arms.
Then they both looked up to see
A shock of blue in the groin of the cloud.

And later,
The dog threw up on your shoes.

No, there was far too much today
To carry
To sleep alone.

Fetch

She snatches a book from the shelf,
Jaw and eyes red toward me,
Rolling down here by the heater,
Tennis ball in my mouth.

Born of humans, he'll come back one.
It's all the poor bastard knows.

Bulfinch's *Mythology* falls to the ground
A thick mat of pages
She is stunned to find
Will not bounce, or even roll.

She noses the rims and remembers
A passage she marked,
Orpheus unslung his magic lyre
And mused Cerberus to a dream
Of hounds, pups sniffing fresh trail.
Stupid dog – three heads and all.

She watches me wondering
How I will lick myself.

Parkway Girl

That girl from the corner store
Is not as sweet as she was.
After that storm,
We shoveled slush until twelve.
After the bleacher girls blew her off
          With a click-clock of their tongues.
After they wheeled out the Welch sisters
          Lumpy stretchers and all.
After that boy from the north side.

She's not nearly as kind, either,
Having had to learn the tax form.
She never made the adjustment
After she heard that brand new Mustang
          Pull doughnuts on her lawn,

Having seen the mechanic
          Three times this August
She's harder on the brake and the gas.

Nor is she
Nearly so young or so beautiful.

The House of Moses

When the subway leavens
High tide of workers
From Queens, from Brooklyn, The Bronx,
Down Delancey, down Rivington,
Onto the asphalt estuary
It is morning again
At the matzo factory where
Dominicans, Italians, smart-mouthed
Bay Ridge girls, the indomitable Hasidim
Make their first hard creak
With the long, long legs of the city
As he unfolds a lap by the curb,
Nodding in Yiddish:
"Better you than me."

The once-again immigrants
Commence their noisy shudder
Of oven doors, percolating heat,
Their morning knock arguing
With forklift skids.
The floors are loose
In first ingredient movements,
"Abe, bring the matzo to the first floor."
As if there was only the one
Giant piece, an island among
Gefilte fish and borscht skip rocks.

Their flow is all the repeated
Code of the sea: the same from afar,
A fresh tidal menagerie up close.
The strange foams
Exchange loud instructions
Then roll to the next wave,
Not quite the same.
The city lulls in their backwash
Like a buoy.

At the end of the day
The many tongues descend, drenched in pickle,
Imagining their newly baked horizon
One motley whole.

As their train leaves
The city is rolled up,
Swept from the street,
Boxed and shipped, quietly
Passed over to the suburbs.

New Year

i.

They might as well have stayed in bed
And spent the day sipping bourbon,
Working off a year of hydration

Writing hastily in their coffee
That nostalgia and nonsense
Are the dim children of optimism.

The country was there in the television,
A giant luminescent ball. One-hundred million
Drunkards clapped for the right to flex some hope.

I stared at the apartment block's vinyl siding –
Something would have to happen. Give me
A flake, shutter, change in pastel hue.

To the rabble of noise behind me
I stood patient, almost ambulatory.
They could have put me in a box

And I would have stared at the seams
Waiting for a new natural law
To cut its teeth on the frame.

ii.

Sparkling wine spilled on my books. 12:01.
The TV was now reporting
Someone exploded their thumb.

Another tripped a can of gasoline
While flailing a cigarette,
Torching his whole damn family sky high.
They might as well have stayed in bed

And spent the day sipping Jim Beam,
Working off a year of hydration

Writing hastily in their coffee
To nostalgia and nonsense,
The limp children of nothing.

AT A WINDOW

A moth finds a trap where there is none
Near the corner of my storm window.
He's flying spider on the brain,
Bouncing off the glass,
The way in his way out.

He dashes one dried fleck
To the next, connecting each dot,
Starting again, headstrong.

Perhaps not so much mad as human
His unblinking has the look of direction.
He seems heartened by the way
My plate shocks his flutters,
Pilate to his devotion.

He catches me dozing
And segues with a grin,
Raising his wings
Like tiny preacher's hands,
Forgetting for the instant
The faithless minute on my side.

TRAVELING CARNIVAL LADY

The dollar entry into your village
Of crooked umbrella hubs,
Each of them a soundtrack all its own,
Each with awkward neighbors,
Is a donation, they tell me,

Worth it, as a painter's worth is drawn in contrasts:
Your death sleigh so close to the merry-go-round
Guided by strings and soft brass,
As if Snow White were trying to hush-hush
Her rabble of drunken gnomes.

Your breath smells of lubricant
As I step up for a look at the levers
Just beyond the orbitron's face.

You stand guard at the gate,
A wedge of taffeta, sweat
And cheap purple makeup.

You gonna look or you gonna ride?

I wonder where you're from,
On how many church lots
You've planted these hairy nomads,
Whether you know
The figure the Yak woman cuts
Naked in a parabolic mirror.

The safety bar locks me on autopilot.
My feet stick to the filthy floor.
In the rusted chrome reflection
I get one last look

At the gaps in your mouth.
They know something, don't they?
About my dollar,
A missing pin,
The Devil.

MAN AND WOMAN

Why bother, I wonder, sharing a kingdom?
          Better yet, let's split tracts of ordinary land.
                    Partitioning this country
we might prove affection a child of halves.

For change
          I can attack corners of your empire,
                    hustle sack-wrapped troops
through your gamble of chicken wire,

At my flanks lava breathing mutts,
          thorn-footed pigeons set to tear apart
                    your sheer wings midflight.

You'll return cluster bombs of rosemary
          raised on kites you've knitted from my bulls,
                    committing the neighbors to ally
under a matriarchy of song.

At night I'll grapple from earth to tree
          to your balconies.
                    There study
you as woman,

Virgin while asleep,
          under-ripened in the bed,
                    your stem
I could prune, but it's too early.

Let me pause and drink
          the measure of this battle.
                    On our deathbeds
we'll revisit how you lacked defenses,

How I might have roused you
          on such nights, between battles,
                    with a kiss

or by strangling,

Or worse,
          left you wondering
                    whether I had cared enough
to come again.

Ah, they say, men freeze in grace at puberty
               and here it is, my rude suit:
                         to leave your fists to wonder
pounding away at your headboard.

I could have told you I loved you
               But what would we have done with the time?
               How would we love
Its family room, its TV trays?

This night goes on
          while I order my thinning armaments,
                    planning alone.
Or do you plot, woman?

Sleeping
          you surely foster
                    a coup's larvae.

The Roman's called it
          a malevolent spirit of the dead,
                    though yours, silent,
grows fertile in the quiet

As if the whole of your land,
          from every wild blade
                    to the hen dozing
with visions of morning hatchlings

To the murky water in your pond
          to your fence posts
                    glazing themselves with fog's approach

to the floodlights of your garden,

Saving their energy for other nights,
          when the snapturtles would walk from their shells
                    to greet hibernating winds
and swill their sword tongues on easy barn air,

As if every atom rests knowing
          from visions come
                    the kindle of day
to rouse them to action,

So that even your retreat
          will carry the unbreakable chorus
                    of sisterhood.

I've become so careless with my time
          that with each tick I grow
                    weaker, more soiled,
more demented by war's constructs.

Do you remember
          standing on that boundary
                    where even the fog was tamed
by the spent honey of our differences?

You accepted this plan
          but turned it around
                    buffing it with the old rags of affection.

And so this country has your clean rebel smell, even
          as night lowers its chant over my eyes,
                    your bombing will begin, a melody.

I will stand
Traitor to the cause.

THE THINGS WE LEAVE

Keys, watchband, napkin ring, lost glove,
Vase, socket set, hacksaw blade, luggage trolley.

Pencilholder, businesscard, pen,
Knife, glasses case, candlestick, staple gun...

A CD collection, the cases long having accepted
Strange contents – Miles Davis in a Freddie Mercury
wrap.

The things that serve us like slaves
Erase us when we are gone:

Monopoly pieces, four phones,
Blender, scissor, dispenser, rack,

Laundrybag, cameracase, billfold, bike,
Weddingring-passport-thesaurus-pin

Sit orderly in compartments, steely on shelves,
Uncertain whether they'll be needed again,
When their time will come. If it will.

When mine comes they'll all sit up on their worn knobs,
Balance on tips, on wheels, twirl around in holders,
Clattering in unison:

The old bastard's dead

And, all at once, forget.

Water

MORNING PEN

The sun I keep drawing
Blots the dew's clear ink,
Dawn still stuck
Up a barrel of dark.

RAIN

*At any street corner the feeling of absurdity can strike any man in
the face.* Albert Camus: *The Myth of Sisyphus*

He is wringing out his eyes
Trying to drown me again
Before I can cross East 10th
To the Korean on the Avenue.

There's his henchman goon,
Leo "Seven Fingers,"
His only thumb vicegripping a cigar.

There are others too, I suspect.
The launderer with his bleach bombs,
Heroin kid posing as twiggy tree,
Mercedes stuffed with gangster eyeballs,
The ravioli woman, a cannoli for a blow gun.

He doesn't even think I've noticed
The lightning rod stuck to my shoe.

PROMETHEUS

The first snap of cold
against skin.
        How were we?
Naked to be sure,
grazers of boneless wind.
        What happened?

Maybe we stumbled onto
an invisible playing field.
The teenage gods
were practicing their weather.
Zeus was hitting out thunderbolts.
"Catch this you little freaks!"

They watched as we learned
to build things that would cover us,
to imitate the uterine tunnels and caves.
For a time we were warm again.
But they got better with their equipment,
surer in their stances,
curveballing the cold through the cracks
to explode its tendrils on our beds.

Until one day wandering the field
we came to an empty locker,
unlocked, carved in blackened oak,
the words *P - 23 Defensive Titan*.
Inside were two rocks
which we pounded together
as some of us dreamed the gods did,
and welcomed the fire spirits
with fat, dumb mortal fingers.

A roar fell from the mountain.
"Prometheus? You bastard!"
We dropped hunks of seared meat on our laps.
Inside the elders were already teaching us to knit.

History crackled, burst into flame, seasons.

TWIN PEAKS

If I told you
The fog was escaping
With stolen breath of trees
Or that his eyes seemed
Cut from bedsheets,
Streaming past us a ghoul
Late for his afternoon séance,

You would have pointed
To his safe reaches, the liquid cotton
Dancing like a healing man's smoke
Around an assembly of the faithful,
Their hair crowned in a heady
Amalgam of sugar and mist.

I would have said
His darkened belly warned of thunder,
Twitching your dog's nose
While she barked, just once,
Figuring not to run and catch him
But hide in your pant leg.

I would have seen the wind
Swing our fog like a bag of rocksalt,
Pummeling tourist windshields,
While you draped him

Around hood ornaments
as a halo of good will.

I watch his tattered pelvis
Stretch its wet reptilian spine,
The pitch-forked tail
Slit the palms down Dolores Street,
As you make strips of sunlight
Rainbow pigeons down to the valley.

And there is more you see:
Hobo legs, shoes ridiculous,
Hobbling over apartment block props
Set up for this giant clown
To hop-dance-twist-keel over on,
Grinning with a bow.

THE THING

Does it come with faithfulness?
If so, my pen holds it
Four-fold over me;
The gear shift on my motorcycle
Is as loyal as the staff of Moses
At full prophecy.
Did Kennedy,
Philanderer and faithful servant have one?
(And did he lose it?)

I wonder whether hard work earns it,
Or character.
Did Armstrong blow one in his cheeks?
Do farriers grow them on their triceps?
Did Atlas plant some where he walked?
Does it smell like incense
Or a cedar crate in Vermont spring?

Is it an invisible dog print on asphalt,
Whose presence is suspended by imagination?
Or does imagination miss it altogether
There in the empty water bowl?

Can it be held or traded like cash?
Is there a dealer, a school marm who hoards it,
Doling it out as discipline?
Or is she a nymph teasing it from vine hair
To a few feral wanderers.

Is it in the space behind my bookshelf
Collecting dust?
(Will the cockroaches want one?)

Is it
In a word?

Early December

My uncle had just returned with the tree
Frozen as cold as the ground.
The Christmas fish was left out thawing.
Our dog licked olive oil from the floor.
"Snow's comin', I hear."
He tugged off his jacket.

It took about five snow driveways
Before December started paying for itself,
And even then it fell a luke choice
Between the weatherman's glow
And broken relatives
Spinning like Yuletide soundtracks
On the family room rug.
I was thinking

How early we got our trees,
Where you would get one
Even if you didn't live in Jersey,
The way the needles stabbed you
When dragging it to the street
The day after New Year's.
How long the neighbors would
Leave out their plastic Santas.

In the yard we found the snowman's garb,
Listening for the sound
Of his first winter coat.

BACKYARD ORPHEUS

Old Uncle Ferdinand's ears
    started to disappear
        on a birthday last spring
when he took off his hat, the first time in months.

No one could name the cause,
    or any cause in the family,
        for even his brother
when he died years before, ears like tree stumps.

Whatever it was, we talked about the way
    it cut out around the borders
        a green brown, the shape
oak leaves curl to in early summer.

We watched them melt into funnels
    spotted with ripened pimples,
        little planters holding thick
gray hairs, as if the house spiders had gone mad.

He used them to cup the walls,
    eavesdropping on nature.
        Through the brick-faced kitchen
he could hear behind the bark of trees ants stepping in circles,

Marching out the days
until the vanishing, its many reasons
were complete.

Ours was a freakshow
of hilarious missing parts.

THE ROSE

Its truss rod sure enough.
Bitter green stalk below rivals
Any stalk, the leaves
Precise as math book problems.
The thing reeks like dead poets.

Petals when ripped
Quickly swell to mask
White edges ashamed of white.
(They will not squelch to rectangle;
Tomorrow the bits will twist maroon.)

Crimson blotches recall bodega plastic.
The cigarette packs were in perfect order
Even after their unwrapping,
But the plant resists flattening,
Curls itself double
As if to lead a quick reform.

Veins stamp like fingers
Leavening flesh. The rose is shallow,
Precise in its mockery of form,
And in its perfect form - plucked for scrutiny -
Teases belief from our pupils,
Precisely aculeate, plotting, deadly,
Though edges reveal venomless white attar.

Neither silken nor sure
In its guise the rose fools only the true.
Upon waking false lovers
Quit to their own beds to sleep,
The deception plain in daylight.

The curve seeks perfection
Toward the base where there is more
To inspect:

Inner peddles coddling pink fetuses;
Yellow spawns inside waiting
There alone, confused
In their invisible stasis.

Ripped again, it triples its folds
Calling out in mockery
"I will continue my honey lull,"
Remontant ad infinitum.

Long before its songs became boring
The rose was lost completely
In the looking, its own politics.

HOUSE WIFE

Cool wind
    Stuck in the vase
She forced room on the mantelpiece
    She has not dusted since June
When the photographer showed
    When she laid rose petals across wood
Handsomely carved at forty years
    Borrowed from the rectory
Fingerprints still crisp
    When the young minister died
Hands as thin as bookmarks
    He liked to sit with the back door open
She managed to ignore all summer
    That strange crackling in the fireplace
The skulk of handymen storming her nave
    The porch door locked and shut
It was time to kindle the fire
    To flirt with the screen
A whisper one more time
    His kiss of breeze
To be her last

ENTRANCE

for Erin

You first saw her borders,
Dimensions unsketched.
A slick gray wax of a moon,
Your eye wider than Earth.

She climbed out of a Memphis elm
Holding a pigeon (Or was it a dove?)
Wide mouthed as if she wanted
To swallow whole your discovery,
Erase your moments together
Before the clatter of opinion
Showed up to pencil in
The continent's struggle of heavy spines,
Its scratched-in mountains,
The panting shores.

It began at once to carve her river strangeness
In fiery ornaments haunted by the holler of boys
From the dirty glass of pickups.
They began, at once, to map the structure of her roots,

Spreading out into colonies
That fingered her still damp liaisons.
The woodworkers held a lathe to her perimeter
Splintering the quiet lines.

Instead of her face you found
The many-headed social beast
Whipping his prying lashes,
Mocking your simplicity
While you groped for your lost eye

In letters, old boxes, among jewelry dust,
For the chance to see her alone.

Lime

BUILDERS IN TOMS RIVER

The builders stood at sunset
Knotted beams to the skinless house,
Waiting in their wallboard film
For a pile of framing nails to go.

They wore the workboots of the continent,
Stained by turpentine, smelling like basements,
A six-pack of Bud in August
More to them than a thousand ice ages.

These were architecture's bottlenecks
Scaffolded by shingles and attic ducts,
Building their houses as if to store
Grout bags, power tools, the site's cool breath,

As if the only domestic voices
Would be echoes of misfired nails,
Drops of stale coffee
A mutter about union dues.

Light bottomed. The builders stood in a circle
Aiming their hammers like fingers
To blame the rooftops
For living beyond their age.

The Art

The building of the lofty rhyme is like any other masonry or bricklaying: we have theories of its rise, height, decline and fall — which latter, it would seem, is now near, among all people.
Thomas Carlyle: *Critical and Miscellaneous Essays*

Life is hard
is the lesson
masons teach their kids
at 6:30 in the morning
loading gravel
onto a dump truck.

He would rock a shovel
like a hoe to the earth
until its blade stiffed
knots of dry dirt.

Hard life was his art
also.
It had its method:
watch your step,
plant your boots,
grip tightly.
Civilization is loose

While you're patching
its foundations,
building its stoops,
floating its walkways.

I'll take this pen,
balance it,
mark my ground,
and hold on.

JEALOUSY

Helen Keller: *The Story of My Life*

Trunk, branch, fruit:
We're still family aren't we?

Your seeds will mingle
With my free marrow
Until strong enough
To stand on my chest.

Breaking earth and skyline
Your kiss of green
Shades me to old age,

Cutting the air in murmurs,
In familiar songs,
As if you've known
My name all along,
The pet sounds
My mother hum-sang.

Do you not hope
To be like me,
Forcing your bark
In sinuous twists
That mimic, crackle, thrust
Upward from your roots,
Creak your knotted limbs?

I wonder what you're up to
In your old age,
Ceasing to spring
Apple, orange, fig.
Do you feel abandoned
As I've moved on,

Left to your own deformities,
To the shock of winter?

Or are you waiting for me
To splinter and die?

(Soon, soon.)
To green your young
On the seasoned matter
Of my heart.

ON LEAVING

We asked for the seasons:
A libertine spring,
A pregnant fall,
A winter on whose carpet we could wane.
Until the seasons refused
To do anything at all.

We saw the sun to the west
As bald and crazy as the moon,
In postcards and on the television,
So we started westward.

We asked for cool lakes
The size of small oceans
Without their retribution,
For stretched midlands
Their waif bellies, their solid horizons,
And went to thresh in that palette.

We grew fat in thick woods,
Our voices squelched
By oak canopies,
By din of night animal run.

We asked for starched canyon
Lands the devil threw up in puberty.
We went there to challenge him.

We asked for the fog and saw it
Pawing the hillside the next morning.
So we moved there.

But it wasn't far enough.
We moved to the hilltop,
To the lip of the rocks,
To the unbreathing trophy of the world

Until salted mezzanines
Coated our nostrils
And brine careened in our stomachs.
Until the continent puttered behind.
When we turned around,
You and I,
To curse a homeless
Beggar sun.

POEM
for E.B.

As many words you'll find on five twenties,
Old ones or the bloated Jacksons,
This oversized postcard
Never earned a penny in its life
Sitting on a metal display,
Face to the grocery wall,
Waiting for a pair of slow eyes.

It came from 1976.
An exit 98 shore town:
Rusted ladder down to the beach
Hoofing sand with steel bottoms
Barnacled from stallion waves,
Sand combed by a blind child
Who could feel away defects.

The sea mouths the picture silent.
So we imagine only human sounds:
Skate on plank, boneless whistle,
The lifeguard rushing from mid-picture
Like a guano cake ornament,
Framed by ancient lamp posts
Painted lumpy silver come May.

Leathery fat lady in pink hawks maps;
Twin boys in bird-print swim trunks
Dagger with blunt ice cream cones;
The mother mouth-stretched in sun hat.
Her husband grabs her across the stomach
Where a sweater knots,
Sleeves propelling as she twists.

"Greetings from Avon by Sea"
Arched across a white border at the bottom
Tells of a summer never cooled,
When the shore was creature run,

Scraped by giant crustaceans
Who inhaled an ancient salt,
A whiff of life before fire.

You can almost see it in the photograph
Stirring on the water's forehead.
A murder of horseshoe crabs
Raise a brine-encrusted army,
Their armor a boardwalk of wet helmets.

The photographer has waited a million years
For life to land again.

END OF THE WORLD

for Charles Simic

My aunt predicted the end
Of your establishment, you cretins.
She was picking burs out of the dog.
The TV was on.
Rain flattened the tall grass out back.

Reagan gave his second inaugural,
A fresh-cut buzz lumping his head.
There were cheers, stomps, one catcall.
"I could have shaved him for twenty bucks – cash."
(My aunt groomed dogs in her garage.)
The antenna went out.

My uncle arrived a commute of wet rubber and khaki.
She mixed him a drink on cue.
One good martini was better than a dozen Iran-Contras.

The television hurled a snowball into his ear
As he plugged it into the kids' room,
Whacked it a good one with his boot and left.

"You're slicker than the rain, Ronnie."

TO BRUEGEL THE ELDER
After the Wheat Harvest

Call me Simon, one of your figures or all.
(You did not bother separating wheat from wheat.)
Grounded here, a sack of lumpy grain,
My tolerance for work is steady as my snore,
Its chorus all grainy diminuendo.
Born of the elements, my brother Cain does all

To forget he has traded summer for sure bounty.
No longer a spiky youth threshing in the field below
The work has grown his body south, his head a pale fruit
Sacrificed by twin shoulders set like scythes in granite
Femurs, skin, and muscle, a stern report
Of earth-stripped hat and jug.

He's gone hard and dry as the pitchfork handle -
Even his midday meal is a risk to the harvest.
His commands only move the carrying along,
Uttering directions, milestones in the work,
Firm, reverent geographies:

Procession of carriers hooded as wheat nuns;
A few tepee-shaped outposts;
Twin birds in ascending fervor;
Boats setting off *con sordino* in the humidity;
Lone basket and flat ladder;
A lunch on fodder tied together as benches;
Bread, soup, sweat feeding a knotted tree.

He is coming toward me now, heavy bones
He has used as levers to balance
Between morning and afternoon,
Between grain and field, church and brother.
The priest in the bell tower takes a sip of wine
Admiring the product winding toward town.

Proof that I exist.

JUDGMENT

Tonight the dogs are quiet in their beds.
The moon slides through cracks in the fence,
Scintillating to our neighbor's
Lunatic back and forth with a garden hose.
A pair of sneakers rocks the electric line.

Before tonight the whole block feared
Summer had gone and would never come back -
The lawn wasn't mowed and tilled.
The teenager two doors down ran away.
The Welch twins called the cops on the street cleaner.

But in the garage it is cool.
Sawdust piles mark the quadrants of the room
Just as they were left,
Formed and assured, their labor complete.
The wind reads the bandsaw's literature.

Over the street lamps the mountain presides,
Scratching his greasy beard.
The old natural laws
Lie crib notes at his feet.

Rear View

The headpiece of your car,
Six cars back, three lanes over,
Felt like floodlights, or a ski rack,
Or horns – it was too early to tell,

Even as you swerved left
Ramming forward, changing lanes,
Only a glare caught my eye:
Your giant chrome grill,

One of fifty thousand
Moon-polished Crown Victorias.
I looked at my ashtray. Shut.
I wanted to reached for it but

For the tattle of glass
As I slowed for the Amboy toll booths,
Working my seat depths,
My Ford haggling with the asphalt.

Then it came – a headlight flash
Maybe, or a swatch of sun
High-beaming from the Saturn dealer.
It was too early to tell.

I focused: road lines, a concrete meridian,
My wheels fixed to the parkway.
A bigger wheel had taken over,
Locking me in its centrifuge.

I was a small planet
Orbiting a knock-off Earth
Of cloud-strewn newsprint, dull scissor cut.
The continents below were not right, either.

Land faked land,
India it might have been.
(I was too early to tell.)
Or an Indian with a slim Italian boot.

I saw the continents panting,
Their Himalayan spines wriggling
Like a reptile under a giant black heel,
His pulse forcing tides to reverse.

I searched a few legal truths:
My glove compartment, license, registration.
What else would be stuck?
And something rattled below my cockpit

As your car flitted by,
A white blueplate special,
The side wind finally blowing me off course,
Trunk letters reporting formally

New Jersey State Trooper.

SONG

The gas pump boys, like
cigarettes, have their show
with the light. In company
everything's better.

Take this job –
all the gas a 355 can
handle, and a
six-pack shake
from Omar who
runs the liquor store
and a '72 Eldorado.

Eyes claw the plane
of macadam, sliding
through car windows
prying up skirts and chrome
exhausts, a quick grope
of face painted wet
with brown lipstick.

The pretty girl
smiling in her map
steps forward.
She's heard about them.

On Common Man

Within a narrow circle he feels himself master of his fate, but against major events he is as helpless as against the elements. So far from endeavouring to influence the future, he simply lies down and lets things happen to him. George Orwell: *Inside the Whale and Other Essays*

I, too, sing of war, of the perfect soldier,
A newly minted veteran who imagines

Injured comrades he carried from battle in one arm,
The flannel flags he planted with the other.

Grappling for sturdy ground in the backyard,
He covers in a basement workshop guarding

His medals: the clean rags, unworn neckties,
The nooses of the country jammed in a gift drawer
Without wearer, teacher.

He came to know his enemies –
Tan college sweaters,
The Sanskrit bond report,
His neighbor's tax return,
Simple annoyances
Fleeting as the morning paper.

His archpromises,
Distractions
Laid in sheets of veneer,
Were not enough to kill him
(His days were comfortable),

But intended to maim,
Render him irretrievable.
Their tactics pure stealth.
They came
In cartons of six, in sports sections,
In elections, coffee shop politics, in lawns to mow,

Under a honey cloak of sexy advertisements.

Like the true veteran, his artilleryman's vision
Becomes nearsighted, speckled in optimism.
His belly runs. Full.

And now, at night, each locust croaks a din
Of unavailable mentors who, like night,

Let his potential lie there
A dim alarm clock,
The next pair of shoes,
His third wife,
The sounds of war.

POULTRY SALE

In which the shop proprietor instructs his employees

First order of business:
Two offers just in on Yeats's index finger.
First a trade-in on some cellulite in a jar - Italian -
The other from that sneaky Irishman, Heaney.

There are to be no trade-ins on Irish poets
(This is a business, not a pub.)
But you can bundle Williams' corns.

So, to repeat:
THERE ARE TWO RULES IN MY STORE:

One, you have to keep moving the stock –
Churn-churn-churn-fresh pickle-churn!

Two, remember the rules --
Rhymers sell, the others are for the reviewers.

Don't drink that!
That's Bukowski's liver, idiot.

And how many times do I have to tell you
Whitman's lead shot does not belong in the Plath case!

Move Charles Simic's haunted matchbook,
Hide Neruda's foreskin and Byron's underwear.
They're upsetting the customers.

Could someone please find this man Rilke's ear?